The View from January

The View from January

Poems by

Thomas Allbaugh

Author photograph by Timothy Fielding
Cover design by Shay Culligan

ISBN: 978-1-950462-57-5

Kelsay Books Inc.

kelsaybooks.com

502 S 1040 E, A119
American Fork, Utah 84003

For Michael, in memory

Acknowledgments

Poems from this collection appeared in the following journals:

"Moves" first appeared in *The West Wind*

"Some Lines Nine Months after the Funeral" and "Light after First Snow: 1991" in *Mnemosyne*

"Flying" and "Watching De Maupassant" in *TextLitMag*

"Can You Spare Change," "Archeology of the Treasurer: A Dig," "Paul Bonfiglio's South Side Sweets," and "One for the Fish" in *The West Wind*

"Searching for Stationary" in *Dime Show Review*

"What We Must Do Now" in *The River Heron Review*

"The View from January" in *Whale Road Review*

Contents

Light after First Snow, January 1991

In the aquarium, the goldfish give sudden delight
by the broad health of their fanning fins.
The baby awakes, breathes, smiles.
After she also eats, she babbles.
Soon she will add to the commerce of Babylon.

Delight is found in the circuit,
in things moving as we have seen them move,
as daylight returning on the path
in new country.
There were no rude awakenings,
only the fast-food trash left to the snow,
which should by all accounts,
be here. Roofs across the street
press under grey ice
and on the road
a coast of snow.

And she says,
"You'd think that in Michigan
they'd have this plow business down
like the garbage collection,"
takes the baby
and walks out carefully over the ice.
Car doors close.
Remember how the baby smiled.
On her stomach, she pushed up
to see at a new eye level.
She reached up and her head fell back
to the padded, soft sheet
of the crib.

Flying

If I don't check my luggage at the gate,
flying is the closest I come
to being homeless,
my burden wheeled past
the watchful sidewalk personnel
from corner to
corner, no one to stand over it
while I buy candy or a paper,
worn backpack and identifying tags and ribbons a
sign I am headed out of town, if I can find the exit ramp,
human clinging to shred of dignity
to be rundown by
the mass exit of cars and buses in the coming economic
shakedown that has already dropped
me.

If I have to keep my mouth open the whole time,
the dentist's chair is the closest I come
to being God,
audience to an endless stream of first person
accounts of the hygienist sharing her reading of Custer and
Rod Stewart and how to raise her daughters.
This path out of my own first-person limited monotony,
my mouth-strained-open, transforms into a kind of jaw-breaking,
limited omniscience,
hearing and seeing, if not all, then at least
so much
she has missed.

Archeology of the Treasurer: A Dig

At a strip mall diner table
she transfers from the old purse to the new one
her stash,
this weighty potential for time lost to be found

—like that towing bill we uncovered,
reimbursed by the insurance company and used
for down-payment on her engagement ring—

among the daily specials for frozen yogurt
never bought two years ago,
passes to a home show
and the county fair,
a lost asprin, ticket stubs to movies,
receipts and birth certificates, social security cards, and HMO
cards
for four children,
all exposed to daylight,
the dropping ringing of keys, and the quieter
passport, checkbook, and wallet,
the wad of HMO radiation invoices
folded there in the side pocket,
candy and gum wrappers no longer scented.

Little goes to
the new purse,
soon heavy also
because life tends toward
paths in her way she
celebrates.

Searching for Stationery

I read your letter anyway
and then had to search
for stationery
before writing back.
I do not love or say,
as a habit, these grand things. They
embarrass me.

As I walked, my jeans,
creased to daily living,
like an x-ray or
like the Shroud of Turin,
showed the old wounds.

In the car,
driving, thinking of your letter, I heard, almost, a song,
bottles rolling over jumper cables in the back.
I passed a crowd downtown, on cracked and broken curbs,
gathered
under some foreign policy,
with the other unredeemable things,
holding sway, channeling wind, a temporal
power, stone against and reaching toward
cloud masses.

And I thought,
For those who journey as though at sea
there are songs that come as though from beyond.
With the present already past,
the past always present,
every pain becomes infused
with longing, and always
some suspect
we are fools.

In a rented room, I write
on plain page how you invaded,
brightened my way.
Do we wait? It wasn't always there
when I almost touched you.
I've kept moving, swallowed
all the words I didn't finally say to you about

what we saw practiced everywhere,
what no one but you or I can keep from coming true.

What We Must Do Now

For Michael

What is length of days
but the endurance of sorrows
when to go out for your season
was to see the fragrant and flowering and,
though broken among the broken,
to frame jokes and
healing in friendships before
the light was lost and you
slipped away from us.
Though your choice
includes you no more
always
we will not say you are lost; lost
refers only to us, to our words
shaped to
blame and loss
not carried away
by wind, by time, by
whatever is and will
come.

We go now and mourn
in the days to come that will now not be seen
when you will not stop being ours
held forever
in what remains of this length of days.

The View from January

A friend said this was beautiful,
to imagine that a month offered
vision, as though it were
a platform
over a canyon
we really could find
in our time.

I want to know now,
what was beautiful, I mean,
beyond the phrase,

when the usual came
from the namesake, the two-faced
deity lurking there behind
all our commerce,
and I thought only
of beginnings, of plans,

in the view from January,
missed the ending that came
as you sought to end your
sad young theatre of masks
no one ever tried to look past.

I am always doing that now, looking
past, discovering something else in
the unchanging
turning
face always fixed
except for what keeps disappearing
as the cloud cover passes over the mountain ahead.

To the Sounds in Silence

The old song reminded again,
those D minor charts played for friends,
back then, in those early '70s when neon
still glowed, and now academics half my age
talk about it, get it again,
the hegemonic sounds in the silence made by gender and race and,
beyond the buzzing light,
I finally get it.

Though I never went on to sing—the one thing
I could do—
I had friends who heard me even then,
before the choice of the mediocre college I settled for, where
the unsigned, mutual agreements to ignore the indifference
held all sways in position
until graduation
and no one thought to ask—it was such a strange place—
"Do you sing?"

Today, I use the D minor key for other pursuits, pass
as another no-voice with
the silence always there and
many sounds of
strangers conversing next door,
the guarded elevator looks between dings of floors passed,
inner distant approximations made of my frayed pants cuffs,
water rushing in the building, the ticking of
a parking meter, the daylight hitting of baseballs,
and the insect mute of
iphones,
into sunset.

Lines Written Nine Months after the Funeral

What I say
I say
to myself, into a paper bag, no one
wants it or will attach it to any wall in the
sun or the gently shadowed
walks they know.
Out of season, you can't
give this away.
Out of season,
there are
buildings for these topics
and times,
places, community leaders, pastors,
and therapists, all
specially designated.

Begin here in this
your place, this
basement of walls that held
our childhood and now
holds boxes of awards and
clothes you will not return for.
Let words fall
where no wind will unsay them.

Keep them.
Keep daily the
silence
and give away
the other things—
bread,
information,
art—
if you can.

One for the Fish

There he is,
with net and pail shadowing the rocks over the cascade,
almost ready to dive in among them, to know their life as
method will not allow,
in the sunlight and clouds, where he carries the great category
giving him work
that always began with play
with wading the shallows of the great river running ridiculous and
jagged down all maps,
contouring states
like his great line yet to be drawn in print
between minnow and not-minnow, counting, measuring
fins and colorings,
for the fish,
to establish the
new name,
a new species against all those lost and
a new word

to fill living rooms of square tanks bubbling with bass and lighting,
rooms measured for something inward,
the memory of
the roar of water, the shadow of the boat
against the surface,
all that will not be
named.

Paul Bonfiglio's South Side Sweets

At the stop light,
the Flagg Gas and Food Mart sign with
chipped red letters now presides over weeds protected
by chain-link fence.
I remember being new in town and buying gas there
before the freeway went through, wondering when
I was going to find my real community,
middle aged already, beginning to bald a little,
not really growing anymore but still needing to
keep this from strangers whose smiles I could not read.

And I think about my grandfather's
candy store,
Paul Bonfiglio's South Side Sweets
after the murders.
Does anyone drive by there now, I wonder, and remember when
they stopped in for Alka Seltser or a "river d'green," where he
served in his white button down shirt and

even then, at the end, would not allow his tie
to brush the candy he'd scoop before he learned not to hand the
bag to
kids who refused to pay, who ran after he
could come out from behind the case? He still trusted them
and unlocked the door that last Sunday night, not seeing who was
behind them, behind the corner.

The light turns green. I think of myself, again, driving, except,
was he ready to leave his immigrant life, the way that I am, a bit
younger,
to leave this transient commute to some building where I express
professorial otherness, wondering if years from now
someone will pass and remember

through the weeds, the chipped paint, the chain link fence on some
lost corner,
how I helped them
in some way in
their growth
even if only with a glass of water,
Alka Seltzer, or a "river d'green"?

Smudge: Toward a Devotion

Though I called out to you sometimes,
when my hope,
a wasted smudge of
feathers and bones
could not join,
you came like the wind.
Now I see
you planting me
like a tree
or the grass that covers
the hillside where

you are still the wind, and I still yearn
for other places and probably always will,
though I sometimes hear this nut
cracking, shooting out, doing
violence to the soil, killing it, saying
as below, so above,
living out beneath the surface this dream of trees,
in winter, in summer,
a world above ghosted,
of fowl and water creatures,
insects and local life forms near
rivers, lakes, and streams,

a world in the leaf, a leaf in the world

where villages spring up and people
eventually join the circus.

What is thankfulness? What devotion?
Branches reach up in
forms first seen in earth,
holding out in a thinning air that has not asked
for branches but still swirls about them like question marks spilled
on the page.

Countertop, the Word

Countertop,
the word, a compound,
tonight designates the place
where I pour water
from the coffeepot into the
coffee maker.

Like other nouns,
it is also a reminder of
this act of pouring water,
written in my journal, something about
water for tomorrow's
exile from this act of pouring

but also, more grandly,
a word to become
in you, dear reader
the countertop you picture.

I ask, in this joining, are you/we in exile
from other acts?

Coffee pot—another word—
moves us to pictures, even as
we cannot be sure that they are really
among the True Forms.

Water we can see there, running
along the true banks where the winged horses
drink and pose for poems.

Worse, I haven't told you yet, dear reader,
there are
stains and food stuff
on my countertop.
You never pictured them; I never asked you to.

Ending the Relationship

I'm through with writing novels,
with this exhaustion, this
writing into the middle of
some adult and pointless
matter that resembles
life itself, removing me two times and
which, furthermore,
I have conspired to
make
"real,"
and it will only
again make me aware of
those ghosts of
childhood friends and high school exes
who have not followed me
this far into mid-life,
who dumped me for older
men with moneyed
interests, men they knew would one day not
try to write this novel.

I want to wash my hands of it all,
deny any incarnation,
though they tell me I might
get comfortable with it,
the adult thinking
and the teasing play that
lead to
this, the real muddied interest
of
the world.

Watching De Maupassant

Nearby, two girls made up and bored look out on the concourse,
reminding me that Guy De Maupassant sat in the city square
observing others.
He must have been
a young writer then.

The two girls' people watching is perhaps mixed,
as it is for me, with
wanting to be watched, or at least noticed,
themselves.

Pink and gray sweaters reveal how
they must calorie watch. One has a tan and
the other a brown purse, both have light brown hair,
both are white, with the same small nose.

I'm too old to people watch without getting terrible about it,
and anyway,
I'm not sure what De Maupassant must have seen, or how he saw,
or
if he saw. I only heard
this from Mr. Kouch, my eighth grade English teacher who gave
Reader's Digest
vocabulary tests, also where I learned the meaning of
"ostentatious" before reading
"The Necklace" but I never really connected this story with
people watching. That eight grade year remains now that I

remember Mr. Kouch on my way home forty-five years later
and wonder if these girls have read De Maupassant or
if they got their skills on their own.

To the Next Day

The screen screams the social nasties, manages
clichéd mumbles
of a world in neon lit with adultery and
subterranean trifles beyond
curfew, says "This is ours, for free, the world
we hold,"
believes in bodily digitalized, the world long beyond
possibility.

Morning brings the old medium,
these pages cold in
retreat, these
whispered vowels and voices
yellow, brown in their fall
from trees, leaving for
sidewalks, lawns, and, if you are there,
swimming pools, and finally
for piles and bags mixed in with
cut grass.

Except there is this stray
at my feet
I pick up, and take home,
this news of the unseen yet
in the world.

Know its familiar name, tell it.
Still,
hold out
To know what it has not yet whispered.

Into

I can descend at will
into flesh, bones, blood,
I can drop into the stone and mud and rushing tide
under stars
and other
fluids too, I can become quickly the mote,
the substance between neurons, the fluid between
the eyes, the pus in the boil so that
no one remembers my name, my
personal history or mother's
maiden name

this is who I am/become/hope,
all one where this prime predates
all this controlling semantics, the clothed human

because
at will (nothing else works this way)
I am again
where this arch substance
and the prime mover yet
have new things to say
one to the other,

some new story,
this collapsible clay
into which
I descend at will.

At the New Visiting Hours

When I walk in for the visiting hours,
pass the gift shop run by the senior volunteer group
supporting this soft conspiracy
that I am a tourist to the sick, where
even the disinfectant
spirits reminders,
the nurses
in face masks and others in scrubs
to this zoo without cages or motes separating us.

Somehow, I am on tour
stepping on the elevator and watching my feet,
before I walk in and up close on the
heart monitors, IV, and oxygen lines, watching the rounds,
someone much younger than us now checking
every hour into the night to record
vitals. Later they will go dancing or
home to bed.

I am fine, I say, don't need anything, just
passing through, ambassador of
good will being met by my wife, this greater
ambassador to the country beyond the land of
operating tables, while I constantly
look for the hand sanitation stations.

Instead

After the kids are grown,
and you are not just old but also rotten with lists
and no more excuses to volunteer
at the school where
they will now think you not a father but
a pervert with no more
avenues to what the world
may become—

Instead
sit on a park bench and play the flute,
or vote Republican and get in arguments to
find out what you didn't know. Think of other
things for the days that remain as you let go
of the world you once knew a day at a time,
though you are the last string still holding it near,
though you are the only road left to that
world where there are already many
washouts and landslides.

Can You Spare Change?

he calls out from this shore of daylight, where he's
washed up at a table under
the usual fast food neon
and I bring forth from my pockets
giving the order

"No booze—Get something to eat"
as though the Caesars falling from my hand have power
to make him stand, take up his mat, and walk
into the American Dream

you can't hold
at evening
in greased, worn folds of rags in plastic bags.

Moves

The chess pieces had been spilled
across six days of outlines.
all week long, homesickness wrote
"The sidewalks here are without patterns,"
and cleaned dust from windows
after shadows of branches waved through.

Your last letter needed
no response; there'd been no talk
in several seasons.
But "New place, reading Jung" seemed one suggestion,
"Snowy afternoons" another.

Never noted was the sun
printed on a dream
and burning season-less like art on a
familiar landscape,
except for the stranger,

nor the problem that none of this
could really bring courage.

Traveling Un-parallel Universes with the Friends

On days that follow what would have been your graduation or
your next birthday or
the return of your death day or the
holidays without you again,
the new pain comes in thinking about your friends.
You also left them wondering, you know,
having to move on but wanting to with you still, so that the
one or two things they've said or written
stay with me

especially how they've kept your pictures on
the wall and yelled at them for
having to attend your memorial or not telling them
before it was too late
and now they are going on to new schools, new
arrangements.

When this pain comes
with you always stopped in mid-flight
I realize
so many months are gone, traveled
in the silence of what are turning out to be
universes that are unparalleled.

A poet friend has written of this loss, how
it looks stranger with the years that pass.
To most, the strangeness of it deepens, but
we are left, with time, to
wonder what we could have done.

On Building Believable Characters

To build believable nonfiction characters,
first, wait until everyone you are writing about
is dead. This probably means switching
to eating vegetables, an end to
smoking, drinking scotch,
and driving too fast, unless you are willing
to write glowingly about their contradictions
and their preferences for Buicks
and their arguments against your career choice
at dinner
and your almost-fiancée who told you,
finally, a year in,
that her father was wealthy (You wondered why
you'd never met)
and you were made to watch *Dallas* program after
program with wine commercials and
eventually, in time,
let her call it off.
In the last resort,
if you can't give up beef,
always remember, as you were taught,
that love covers a multitude of sins, which may
allow you to quit writing, which solves
everything.

To build believable fictional characters,
you probably won't need a lawyer, so
start with old crayons, stubby ones
with the paper mostly pulled
away so that the word mauve, for example,
is only a few letters, say mau-or–uve, emblematic
of all you remember now,

that meaningless late November
NFL game on in the background,
not her reasons,
only that
she had turned the game on, even though
she hated football, and left it to distract
from what was really being said
when she explained that it was time,
that iron, fluffy reason that comes to all
and mainly you remember now that
one of the teams in that long ago mud has
for decades
played in another market, and if you mix her up with
another distant lost love, you will be
fine, sin having covered
a multitude of love.

The Seeds of St. Paul

(I Corinthians 15)

They must have been metaphors
he seized on in one moment to
explain something in eternity, something
of the better place, though
the meaning seems harder today.
To build
a life,
more seem drawn
to butterflies.

Today, a small robin, wings tucked in, trotted up
the ramp where my wife
was teaching strings. This was
a year after they gave her
the cockatiel, and on entering where she was
tuning the violins,
the robin was chirping and trotted up to her ankles as though
it knew her, as though it were the UPS
guy with her number and she stopped
to lean down and get the thing to leap
to her finger the way her cockatiel does
at home, the bird they gave her after missing
her son for a few months.

This only got the bird outside to safety
until at the cello, the instrument her son once helped her
fix, the chirping came again, and her colleague said,
"Someone must be wanting to talk to you."

The third time, she began to think
she'd seen this one bird before, and she was
still with the cello, and so the bird led her out
to the tree behind the portable where the flock had
tweeted, as if to say
in the one language they knew,
"See, we are not alone."

About the Author

Thomas Allbaugh's poems, stories, and essays have appeared in many journals including *River Heron Review, Writing on the Edge, Broken Skyline,* and *Relief.* His first novel, *Apocalypse TV,* was published in 2017 and is available from Electio Publishers. He is a professor of English at Azusa Pacific University, where he teaches composition and creative writing.

9 781950 462575